"I just read the first chapter and all I can say is WOW. Why haven't you written this stuff and got it into hands of Christian leaders sooner? I can see myself utilizing this information and teaching it line for line in my Wednesday night adult teaching lessons. You have me hooked for the rest of the book!"

Pastor Phil Corbett,
First Assembly of God, Corrigan, Texas
https://www.CorriganFirst.org

"I've already used one of your chapters in a homily for my parish. I look forward to incorporating these things immediately into my ministry!"

Father Jonathan Goertz,
Our Lady of Lourdes Catholic Church, Henrico, VA
https://OLLRichVA.org

"I have actually used what I learned in reading this book quite a few times!! I found myself in numerous hard conversations with people very close to me, and it showed to be SUCH a better result! I can't stop raving about this book when I use your methods of communication with people who are hurting!"

Natalie Buchanan, Reader

"The book was very impactful to my family: We spent several hours over the dinner table discussing it! Your style is both challenging but also encouraging. You give us practical examples of how to truly minister to hurting people who need the church to be their place of safety. May everyone get this message in them!"

Tracy R. Graham, Reader
https://TracyRGraham.com

"Thank you for putting this book forward. It is a blessing and very needed in transforming this world!"

Aubrey Remedy, Reader
https://AubreyRemedy.com

"Thank you so, so very much! I especially have learned a lot about just being with those who have been wounded. As you say, sometimes, just sitting with them is, in and of itself, ministry. Not jumping in with your own story is so important. THEY are to be the focus! I am thankful for this book!"

Adriene Terrill, Reader

"I was so blessed with reading this! I think it causes those reading it to take a thoughtful look at their life. And it is very readable and applicable."

Jeannine Metzger, Reader

STEWARDING WOUNDED HEARTS

Being Jesus to Wounded People

Dave Wernli

First Day Publishing
Fredericksburg, VA

Table of Contents

To all who have been hurt by the church,
and to all my fellow wounded healers
in the church who see and grieve that hurt.

May we all learn to be
as gentle and truthful as Jesus,
seeing the person behind the wounding,
and reminding them,
maybe for the first time,
who they really are.

Introduction:
Jesus invites wounded people into healing transformation. Do we?

The Problem: We want to help, but we don't know how

When wounded people come into our church, we often (unintentionally) do one of two things:

1. We minimize or discount their pain.
2. We try to "fix" them by being the therapist.

But both just cause more damage. We have the best of intentions. We don't know we're causing damage. And they won't tell us. Because we've made it clear we don't understand their pain. So they keep their pain secret, drawing conclusions like these:

- *"It's not safe to admit I'm hurting in this church."*
- *"I was right; they're judging me. I'd better keep my pain hidden."*
- *"They're all so perfect. There must be something really wrong with me."*
- *"I guess God doesn't love me, care about me, or want me. I'm too broken."*

We thought we were helping. We'd be horrified to know we're causing people to think these things. But too often we are, and they won't tell us. Because, unintentionally, we've identified ourselves as someone who is not a safe person for them.

Often in the Church, we don't understand wounding (and haven't for a long time). But we have to get this right.

Because our churches are already flooded with wounded people. And too many of them are hiding it because they think they're the only one. The truth is too many churches aren't a safe, protected place for people to make their pain and wounding known.

But there's another way.

What this book is

This book shows you:

1. How to create a safe place for wounded people to encounter Jesus, embarking on a life-changing journey of transformation.
2. How to be a safe person, intentionally supporting wounded people on their healing journey.

We will discover what wounding looks like and what wounded people need from you. We'll learn how to steward a wounded person's heart well, supporting the healing Jesus wants to bring.

> ### What does "steward" mean anyway?
>
> To "steward" means to responsibly care for something we don't own.
>
> That's why the Church talks about "stewardship" with regard to finances. It's an acknowledgement that our money belongs to God, not to us.
>
> As the Church, we also have a responsibility to steward people's hearts well. After all, how much more important are hearts than money!

I believe the church today has the right heart. We can do this. We've just never been trained how to steward wounded hearts well, and this book addresses that problem.

As Jesus' hands, feet, voice, and heart to a wounded world, we can become a people that steward wounded hearts well, creating a safe place for wounded people to live out the transformation Jesus has for them, and for us all.

Because if they can't go to the people of God when they're hurting, where can they go?

- 4 -

Chapter 1:
What not to say: Don't minimize, discount, or shame their pain.

Let's get right to it. We're going to start with practical guidelines you can use today: What to say and what not to say.

In this chapter, we'll learn how to stop doing unintentional damage by learning what *not to* say. (In the next chapter, we'll learn how to actually help by learning what *to* say.)

We want to help but don't know how

Many people come to church in silent pain, isolated and hurting. Although we want to help, we can actually motivate them to keep that pain hidden because of the damage we often do when they make their pain known.

We don't know how to help somebody who's hurting. We've never been trained. So unfortunately well-meaning Christians often do more harm than good. We can cause a lot of damage without even knowing it.

Too many churches are not safe places for people to admit they're in pain, whether it's from depression, crippling anxiety, struggles with self-harm or suicide, abuse, post-abortive trauma, or a myriad of other pains and hurts.

And it's not just the unsaved coming into our churches who are hurting. There are large numbers of people in our churches right now who are hurting. But they are hiding their hurt for two reasons.

First, they think they are the only one: *"Look at all these happy people. I'm the only one who's faking it."* But they aren't. The truth is half the people in the room are faking it.

Second, they are afraid of being judged. They have been judged in the past, or they've seen other people with similar issues be treated as "less than."

So our lack of understanding is actually preventing people from getting the healing Jesus has for them. And that's the last thing any of us want.

> ***If they can't go to the people of God
> when they're hurting,
> where can they go?***

Proverbs 18:21 says, "Life and death are in the power of the tongue." What we say and don't say is extremely important.

When we don't understand what wounded people need from us, we can unknowingly communicate judgment and condemnation. This guarantees they will never let another Christian know their hurtful secret. That's not our intention at all. But that is the result.

However, when we understand the nature of wounding, we can communicate love, understanding, acceptance, and compassion. This facilitates the healing Jesus wants to bring into their lives.

The Power of the Tongue
James 3:2-10

[2] We all stumble in many ways. Anyone who is never at fault in what they say is perfect, able to keep their whole body in check.

[3] When we put bits into the mouths of horses to make them obey us, we can turn the whole animal. [4] Or take ships as an example. Although they are so large and are driven by strong winds, they are steered by a very small rudder wherever the pilot wants to go. [5] Likewise, the tongue is a small part of the body, but it makes great boasts. Consider what a great forest is set on fire by a small spark. [6] The tongue also is a fire, a world of evil among the parts of the body. It corrupts the whole body, sets the whole course of one's life on fire, and is itself set on fire by hell.

[7] All kinds of animals, birds, reptiles and sea creatures are being tamed and have been tamed by mankind, [8] but no human being can tame the tongue. It is a restless evil, full of deadly poison. [9] With the tongue we praise our Lord and Father, and with it we curse human beings, who have been made in God's likeness. [10] Out of the same mouth come praise and cursing. My brothers and sisters, this should not be.

A Brief Look Inside Ourselves

What is our motivation? We want people to stop hurting. That's good. But are we wanting that truly for them, or for us because we feel uncomfortable around their pain?

I admit there have been times when I've said something I hoped would cheer someone up, so the conversation would turn happy again. It was more about me being uncomfortable around their pain than it was about really caring for them. And that's not the way of love.

Is the gospel "Try Harder!" or is it "God loves you. You matter"?

Listen to the common responses I've heard Christians give to people who have just vulnerably shared their struggle:

- "You just need to choose joy!" Translation: "Try harder!"

- "You just need to believe and live the Word!" Translation: "Try harder!"

- "You just need to take those dark thoughts captive to Christ!" Translation: "Try harder!"

- "You just need to forgive!" Translation: "Try harder!"

- "You just need to pray, read your Bible, and worship more!" Translation: "Try harder!"

Yes, we all have choices to make. Yes, no one is arguing against believing and living the Word. Yes, learning to take our thoughts captive to Christ is a skill every Christian needs to learn. Yes, forgiveness is extremely important (more on forgiveness in chapters 6 and 7). And yes, intimacy with Jesus through prayer, Bible reading, and worship is critical.

But what if someone does all those things and more, and they're still hurting? What if they do everything you tell them with all their heart, and yet they still feel the crushing blackness of all their pain?

I think many of us would tend to say, "Well, you have to fight for it! You have to contend!" And then we'd quote them some verse about God's faithfulness. Translation: "Try harder!" And the truth is, for many of us, we get very uncomfortable about now, because what we thought should be working isn't working.

The nuance is that those things are all true. God is faithful, and we do need to contend. But that's not what they need to hear right now. That's not how to be Jesus to them right now.

We need to understand WHY all the good, solid, Biblical advice and scripture we're quoting at them isn't working.

The Wrong Answer: "They aren't doing it right!"

The obvious (but wrong) answer is, "They're not doing it right!" We think if they were doing it right, these things would work. So we conclude they must not be doing it right. And we tell them to try harder in all of the Biblically accurate, kind, but self-righteous ways we can muster.

There's a natural reason why we do this. We want our world to be safe. Say something terrible happens to our neighbor's child. We search for a reason to believe they were bad parents. Or the dad is an alcoholic. Or the mom is whatever. Something negative. Because if we find that negative, and we avoid it ourselves, then we can secretly believe the bad thing that happened to them won't happen to us. Our world is safe.

The problem is, that's false security. The truth is a lot messier and uncomfortable. The world is not safe. Bad things, completely out of our control, happen to us all. Granted, we can certainly inflict consequences on ourselves with bad choices and foolish behavior, but trauma done to a person is never their fault.

The Right Answer: God's Up to Something Different

Here's the counter-intuitive secret of why quoting the Bible verses and all the good Christian principles doesn't always work. Ready? Here it is. God's not letting them work. *What?!? God's not letting his own Word work? That makes no sense at all!*

Hang with me a minute here. Let me explain. If God allowed quoting the Bible verses and doing "all the things" to relieve the pain, we'd never search for deeper healing. There's something else God wants to do in their lives. Some deeper level of healing he wants to bring. Some deeper level of anointing he wants to give.

Maybe there's wounding embedded deeply in our heart because it happened so early in life, maybe even before we learned verbal language. Often, we come out of the womb with emotional and spiritual wounding. Or our wounding is the result of someone doing something harmful or traumatic to us very early in life. That's not our fault. The sin done to a child is never the child's fault.

Our responsibility is the judgments we make afterward and the lies we believe about ourselves, about God, about others and how they will treat us, as a result of our wounding.

Can we be born with wounding?

Yes, we can be born with emotional and spiritual wounding. Although out-of-scope for this book, here's a QR Code to a free PDF with three common examples.

https://IdentityInWholeness.com/born-with-wounding

That early wounding can manifest in our lives in a lot of different ways; unfortunately, some of them are less socially acceptable in Christian circles than others. Depression, for example, is often shamed in the church, and that's an injustice we need to correct.

Please don't get me wrong. I'm not saying to ignore or sugar-coat stuff in someone's life. But I am saying we need to accept the person without judging their pain.

**Meet people where they are,
without judging where they are.**

5 things NOT to say that discount their pain

Too often, we unintentionally discount people's pain, minimizing and devaluing it. But when we devalue someone's pain, we devalue them, even if we don't mean to.

The following are five things well-meaning Christians often say, but are not helpful because they discount the person's pain. (We'll cover what to say instead in the next chapter.)

1. "I understand."

No, we really don't understand. Most of us have never experienced what they're going through. And even if we have, we haven't experienced it as them, with their backstory, their fears, and their previous hurts.

They are a different person and are experiencing it differently than we would. Our backgrounds and make-up are different. Our needs are different. Our support system is different. So, no, we do not understand.

When we say, "I understand," we minimize their pain. We trivialize what they're going through.

2. *"I went through something similar…"*

This is not the time to tell our story. Listen to and validate their story. Launching into our story, when they are trying to tell us theirs, minimizes their story and discounts their pain.

They don't need to hear our story. They need us to hear theirs. In their pain, their heart needs to speak and be heard. They need us to listen and make sure they feel heard.

They need us to hear their heart. Typically, when the other person is talking, we aren't really listening. We're politely waiting to talk. **Be a real listener. Don't be a wait-to-talker.**

When we share our story, we take the focus off of them and put it on us. We're telling them, "Your experience is common. I went through it. I got through it. You will too." While that sounds great on paper and may even be true, that's not what they need to hear right now.

They need to hear that they were heard. They need to hear that their pain is legitimate, and we're not shaming them for it.

After we validate their pain (see the next chapter), after they feel heard, then we earn the right to ask them if we can share our story. (Don't presume, *ask*.) At the right time, our story might truly be helpful to them. But keep it short. They don't need all the gory details. Get the focus back on them as soon as you can.

3. *"You'll get through it."*

We are trying to be encouraging, but this just minimizes their pain. Rightly or wrongly, what they conclude from hearing us say this is, "No one understands me, my pain, what I'm going through, or how scared I am. And it's not ok for me to tell them. I better hide it." And that's not the result we want.

4. *"Just have faith."*

When we say things like this, we are unintentionally shaming them for having the pain. Whether we mean it or not, they hear condemnation:

- "They think I'm a bad Christian because I'm going through this."
- "If I had faith, I wouldn't have this problem."
- "I'm trying as hard as I can to have faith, but I still struggle with this. I guess there's no hope for me."

5. *"God's got this."*

While very true, this totally discounts their pain. Whether we mean it or not, what they hear is, "You're wrong to feel bad about this. Why are you so upset? Relax, God will work it all out." While a great thing to tell ourselves when we're going through painful times, don't say this to others. Whether we mean it this way or not, it comes across flippantly.

Avoid "spiritual bypassing"

Many of the examples above are what we call *spiritual bypassing*: Putting a "spiritual band-aid" on a much deeper problem. Spiritual bypassing is quoting a quippy platitude, or even a Bible verse, to "help them feel better," without addressing the deeper issue and the pain they are feeling.

For example, quoting Romans 8:28 at someone, while very true and a powerful verse, can be hurtful when someone is grieving a loss, like the death of a child, the ending of a relationship, loss of a job, etc. Do you see how this minimizes the pain they're going through?

> Romans 8:28
>
> We know that in all things God works for the good of those who love him, who have been called according to his purpose.

Please don't get me wrong. There is a time to share scripture. But it is important to validate their pain first.

Often, our real motive is to help us feel better, because we feel uncomfortable around their pain. But if we're going to support the healing transformation Jesus wants to bring, we need to get comfortable sitting with people in pain.

Practical takeaways from this chapter:

- We can unintentionally do a lot of damage if we don't understand wounding.
- The gospel is "God loves you. You matter," not "Try harder!"
- Meet people where they are, without judging where they are.
- Don't say these 5 things that discount people's pain:
  1. "I understand."
  2. "I went through something similar…"
  3. "You'll get through it."
  4. "Just have faith."
  5. "God's got this."
- Be a real listener. Don't be a wait-to-talker.
- Avoid spiritual bypassing. Don't quote platitudes or even scripture superficially without first understanding the deeper problem.

Don't discount, shame, or minimize their pain. Instead, validate their pain by really hearing their story.

Chapter 2:
What to say: How to validate their pain.

We Heal in Community

We are designed by God to heal in community. Not a big, giant community. I'm not talking about telling hurtful secrets to the whole world or publicly in front of the whole church. Yes, God calls some people to do that, and God does use those stories.

But God does not call most people to do that, because unfortunately too many people in the general congregation don't have a framework for stewarding personal stories. They aren't safe people to share painful stories with because they don't know how to steward them well. And the tender parts of someone's heart revealed in their story deserve to be stewarded well.

So not everyone needs to know everything. But someone needs to know everything. In a small, safe community of other believers, even if it's just one other person, there is real healing power in having our story received.

As the Church, Jesus' hands, feet, mouth, and heart to a wounded world, it's important for us to learn how to receive people's stories and steward them well, honoring the tender and wounded parts of their heart. We can facilitate powerful healing in their lives by simply receiving their painful story with grace. When we steward their story well, we steward their heart well.

To that end, to steward their story well, we need to witness two seemingly obvious but incredibly powerful truths:

1. Witness the painful truth of their story, that this was truly a painful experience for them. This communicates that you see them.

2. Witness that what they experienced was wrong. This communicates they have value.

What does it mean to "be a witness?"

In this context, "being a witness" generally means acknowledging something is true. But it's stronger than that. Wounded people need more than just a general acknowledgement, more than just a polite head nod. Their ears need to actually hear the words coming from your mouth. They need to hear the truth spoken. That's what I mean by being a witness.

"Do you see me?"
Be a witness to the painful truth of their story.

Having someone else acknowledge the pain of their story is amazingly healing.

- "That must have really hurt."
- "It wasn't fair you had to go through that."
- "You are not being treated right by your ex."

- "She should not have said that. That must really hurt to hear. It isn't true."

Just that. Just having someone acknowledge the pain. That's how a heart screaming to be heard starts to heal.

Now please don't get me wrong. This isn't a pity party. This isn't a celebration of victimhood. This isn't trying to "fix it" for someone.

This is a healthy, godly, loving community saying, *"I see you. I see the pain you have to walk through. But you don't have to walk alone. I'll walk with you."*

It's about holding a safe space for the other person to be vulnerable. To let their guard down. To share their story. To be heard.

And this is incredibly healing because most likely when the pain happened, they weren't heard. Often, when the trauma occurred, their voice was shut down and ignored. Just hearing their story and acknowledging their pain without judgment can bring major healing to their heart.

"Do I have value?"
Be a witness that what they experienced was wrong.

To hear someone else say what you experienced was wrong is tremendously freeing and healing, especially in cases of abuse. Abuse communicates, "You have no value, you're just an object for my use." Witnessing that what they experienced was wrong, actually letting them hear you say it, restores their value.

Abuse is never, ever, the victim's fault. No one ever deserves to be physically, mentally, emotionally, or spiritually manipulated, gaslit, or abused. Never.

Just to hear someone say, "It was wrong that you were treated that way," can be tremendously healing.

- "It was wrong that your voice was shut down."
- "It was wrong that you grew up without a dad."
- "It was wrong that they made fun of you."
- "It was wrong that she hurt you like that."

When we're listening to someone's story, we often don't think to say this because it's so obvious. We're busy thinking about the advice we're going to give them after they're done telling their story. But they don't need our "fix." They need our witness, our acknowledgment that what they experienced was wrong.

Have you ever known someone who keeps telling the same story and, even after a long time, seems to be stuck there? *Why can't they just get over it?* Because they're looking for a witness. They desperately need to hear someone else say that what they experienced was wrong.

Of course it was wrong; it's so obvious it goes without saying. No, it doesn't. It needs to be said because it needs to be heard. By them. By their ears. By their heart. Saying it out loud, letting their ears physically hear you say it, speaks directly to their heart. That's what they need. We can learn to supply that. It's such a simple thing and is so powerfully healing.

But what if they're just wallowing in victimhood to get attention and never actually do their own work?

Occasionally you'll find a person always sharing the hard stuff to get attention. Or because they're living in victimhood, looking for their next rescuer, because they've burned out their last one. Here's a QR code to my blog post *"How to Help Someone without Rescuing Them."* The post also has a link to a great video by Danny Silk called *"How to Really Help Someone with a Problem"*.

https://IdentityInWholeness.com/how-to-help-someone-without-rescuing-them/

Key points:

- Codependency is working harder on someone else's problem than they do.

- You can't help someone who doesn't have a problem. Don't waste your emotional energy trying to help someone with a problem they don't admit they have.

- Specific questions to ask that puts the empowerment and responsibility for solving their problem on them.

Acknowledge their pain with reflective listening

When someone shares their pain with you, don't judge it, dismiss it, or minimize it. Reflect it back to them in your own words. Some examples of good things to say are:

- "So do you feel like …?"
- "I'm so sorry you're going through this. That must really hurt."
- "Tell me more about that."

This is not a politician's hollow "I feel your pain" so they can manipulate a vote out of you. This is an honest attempt to truly listen and hear, not only what the person said, but how they feel.

And the beauty of it is that you don't even have to be right. By reflecting back what you thought you heard, even if you got it wrong, you communicate that you're trying to hear their heart. And that communicates value, safety, and acceptance. It makes you a safe person. And a safe church is made up of safe people.

8 Great Things to Say

Here are eight examples of things you can say that make the other person feel heard and create a safe space for them to share and seek healing.

1. *"Tell me more about that."*

This is a great default when you don't know what else to say. It communicates you care, their story is not a burden, and they have value.

2. *"I can't even imagine what you're going through. It must be really hard."*

This is very validating; it invites them to share their feelings. It communicates you care and you're listening.

3. *"You're really brave to face this."*

This can be so powerful. Believe me, they feel anything but brave right now.

4. *"That must really hurt."*

Again, an invitation to share their feelings, hurts, and fears.

5. *"So do you feel like…?"*

Take a guess at how they're feeling. It doesn't matter if you're right or not. Just the fact that someone is trying to understand how they feel is validating. This communicates, *"Someone sees. Someone hears. Someone cares."* Huge.

6. "You're not a bad Christian for going through this."

You may see tears with this one. Because believe me, the enemy, and sadly other Christians, have told them they are. And they are probably telling themselves they are.

7. "I don't know what to say. But I'm here for you."

It's great to admit you don't have all the answers. This validates them as a person because then they don't have to feel condemned for not having all the answers either.

8. "Thank you for sharing this with me."

Such a simple, obvious thing to say, but it can be so powerful. It affirms the value of what they shared. It communicates that hearing their painful story wasn't a burden but a privilege. And that communicates their value as a human being.

Practical takeaways from this chapter:

- Verbally acknowledge the painful truth of their story.
- Let them hear you say that what they experienced was wrong.
- Use reflective listening.

- 8 great things to say:
    1. "Tell me more about that."
    2. "I can't even imagine what you're going through. It must be really hard."
    3. "You're really brave to face this."
    4. "That must really hurt."
    5. "So do you feel like …?"
    6. "You're not a bad Christian for going through this."
    7. "I don't know what to say. But I'm here for you."
    8. "Thank you for sharing this with me."

Because validating their pain is more healing than your solution to "fix their problem."

Chapter 3:
Never judge a person's wounding before you know their story.

Too often in the Church, we try to address the bad fruit in a person's life without taking the time to understand the wounding that caused it. If we're just dealing with the visible bad fruit in people's lives, and not the bad roots in their hearts that cause it, we're just offering a sin management service. *No, thank you.* I want transformation.

Even if we successfully eradicate the visible bad fruit from their lives, but don't deal with the underlying roots, those roots will just cause that bad fruit to pop up somewhere else. We need to address the motivation. We need to understand the wounding.

The Bank Robbers' Parable

Two guys burst into a bank with guns. Both fired their weapons into the air and forced everyone to lay down. They robbed the bank and fled. Later, they were caught, tried, and convicted.

They each received the same lengthy prison sentence from the judge. After all, the facts of both cases were the same. They robbed a bank. They both used a gun (a worse legal offense). Although they didn't physically hurt anyone, they both discharged their weapons (again, a worse legal offense). Justice was served like it should be.

Their motivations, however, were completely different.

The first bank robber was motivated by pure, unadulterated greed. *"They have something I don't. I want it. I'm taking it."*

The second bank robber was motivated by fear for his 8-year daughter, dying from a rare and aggressive disease. She needed an expensive treatment, and she needed it now. But he'd just lost his job, his health insurance was canceled, and the treatment facility required insurance coverage or payment before treatment.

Don't get me wrong. His desperation does not justify the crime. The punishment was just.

A judge and a jury don't need to understand the two men's motivations to hand down judgment and punishment, just the facts of each case.

But if a counselor wants to bring healing and transformation to their lives, he must understand the differences between their motivations.

Who do we want to be?

As the Church, Jesus' body, the physical manifestation of his love here on the Earth, who do we want to be?

If we want to be judge and jury, pronouncing judgment, then we don't need to understand a person's wounding. We can bring judgment with just the facts of the case.

But if we want to bring healing by inviting them into a transformational journey with Jesus, then we must understand the person's wounding, and how that wounding has produced bad fruit in their lives.

The counselor isn't going to justify either bank robber's crime. But he is going to address the problems in each man's life differently, because their heart conditions, their motivations, and their woundings, are completely different.

The "Did You Cut Yourself?" Parable

Two people arrived at the ER with life threatening cuts across their wrists. Although they didn't know each other, their wounds were remarkably similar.

They both received the same life-saving treatment and were discharged in a few hours. Although they both received the same care at the ER, the follow-up care both desperately needed was completely different.

The first person, in his first experience teaching himself to juggle, was trying to juggle sharp machetes. He missed. It was a foolish, careless, accident.

This person needs safety training, with an emphasis on common sense, and a long-term plan for learning to juggle machetes:

1. Start with tennis balls.
2. Then learn to juggle clubs, with your eyes closed, and never drop one.
3. Then move on to machetes, with the sheaths on.
4. Then try it without the sheaths, with medical help standing by.

The second person in the ER that night slit their wrist. It was not an accident. They were intentionally trying to end their life.

This person needs counseling, probably with a professional who understands trauma. They may also need depression medication to keep them stable enough to work through the counseling. They may need inner healing as well.

Both people received exactly the same, identical, emergency medical care. But do you see that in order to prevent a second ER visit, they need completely different follow-up, based on the story behind their wounding?

**Compassion first and truth second,
not truth first or compassion only.**

If someone cuts themselves, too many churches just yell at them, *"Hey, stupid, don't cut yourself! Stop getting blood everywhere, you idiot!"* When we don't lead with compassion, we're too busy passing judgment to bring healing.

And too many churches pretend they didn't cut themselves at all. *"Blood? We don't see any blood? You're fine, no problem here."* When we justify sinful lifestyles, like sex outside marriage, homosexuality, transgenderism, or abortion, we let people spiritually bleed-out by denying the wound behind the lifestyle.

But neither is bandaging the wound like Jesus would, which requires two simultaneous actions:

1. Loving the person.
2. Treating the wound.

Jesus did this perfectly. He set us a powerful example with the woman caught in adultery (see John 8:3-11 on the next page). When the crowd wanted to stone her, Jesus told her, "Neither do I condemn you. Go and leave your life of sin."

He didn't pretend her self-destructive lifestyle wasn't sinful so he could be inclusive. But he didn't meet her with condemnation either. He loved the person without condoning the sin.

The problem is not so much a person's sinful lifestyle as much as it is the wounding that lifestyle is medicating. People trapped in a sinful lifestyle are living out of their wounding and out of the false identity that wounding gave them.

Their initial wounding was likely not their fault; it's something a sinful world did to them. That doesn't minimize their responsibility for subsequent bad choices. But it helps us lead with compassion.

If we want to facilitate the healing transformation Jesus wants to bring, we need to learn how to look beneath the surface. The bad fruit is rarely the actual issue. The root causing the bad fruit is the issue.

John 8:3-11

[3] The teachers of the law and the Pharisees brought in a woman caught in adultery. They made her stand before the group [4] and said to Jesus, "Teacher, this woman was caught in the act of adultery. [5] In the Law Moses commanded us to stone such women. Now what do you say?" [6] They were using this question as a trap, in order to have a basis for accusing him.

But Jesus bent down and started to write on the ground with his finger. [7] When they kept on questioning him, he straightened up and said to them, "Let any one of you who is without sin be the first to throw a stone at her." [8] Again he stooped down and wrote on the ground.

[9] At this, those who heard began to go away one at a time, the older ones first, until only Jesus was left, with the woman still standing there. [10] Jesus straightened up and asked her, "Woman, where are they? Has no one condemned you?"

[11] "No one, sir," she said.

"Then neither do I condemn you," Jesus declared. "Go now and leave your life of sin."

Practical takeaways from this chapter:

- Addressing the bad fruit in someone's life, without dealing with the underlying wounding that caused it, is just sin management.
- Jesus is calling the church to be an agent of transformation.
- Jesus modeled compassion first, truth second.

Lead with compassion. Never judge a person's wounding before you know their story.

Chapter 4:
Never expose someone's shame; that convinces them shame was right.

"I know what's wrong with you, Betsy, you're shamed-based!" -- A "friend" to Betsy Kylstra, co-founder of Restoring the Foundations, after this "friend" returned from an inner-healing conference, where she apparently dialed-in all of Betsy's problems, but none of her own.

To help wounded people, we must understand shame.

If we're going to steward the hearts of wounded people well, we need to understand shame. Because wounded people feel it. They may not know they're wounded, but they know they feel shame.

Shame is the enemy's main weapon to keep them isolated, stuck, broken, and hopeless. And it works all too well.

Wounded people long for authentic community, as we all do, but shame keeps them terrified of it. They long to be known, accepted, and loved. But they live in terror of being known, exposed, and rejected.

And the truth is, we all feel this way. Entering into a community where we can be vulnerable, where we can safely expose our wounding, is a tremendous risk.

We have probably all been hurt in church. And the hard truth is most of us have probably hurt others in church, even though we didn't intend to and we didn't know it.

It's critical that we understand shame, recognizing it when we see it, so we can create a safe space for people to reveal their wounding without getting shamed for being wounded.

Shame is the world's largest prison.

The most secret prison in the world isn't in some sub-basement of a 1960s era non-descript government building within some closed dictatorial regime. But it is also the most populated prison in the world. *"Wait a minute, that doesn't even make sense!"* you say. *"How do you keep the largest prison in the world secret?"*

Put it in the human heart.

That's what shame does. Wounded people often live in the secret prison of shame. Outwardly they look fine. You would never know, by design. But inwardly, they're a swirl of fear and self-hatred, believing lies that drive them underground.

Every human being, including you and me, is affected by shame. It robs us of who we really are, who God created us to be. Shame sets our life on a trajectory of desperately trying in vain to numb its pain.

Some people medicate their shame because the pain of the addiction hurts less.

Some people repeat their shame, wrongly believing the shame from the last failed relationship will be healed by the next one. So we repeat the act we're ashamed of with our inner psyche vowing to get it right this time.

Some people pretend their shame doesn't exist under the false belief that if I act like I'm fine long enough, maybe I'll actually believe it myself.

None of these desperate attempts to quell shame's pain work long-term. Although providing some short-term relief, eventually all the coping methods just add more shame.

But there's good news.

There is something that will work. Or rather, someone (Jesus) that will work. But to understand the victory, we first need to clearly understand the problem. What really is shame, anyway?

Shame is not guilt.
There's a subtle but important difference.

What's the difference between shame and guilt?

Guilt, or conviction, is what the Holy Spirit gives us because he loves us. It's a gift from God. He uses it to correct our sinful behavior because (1) it's self-destructive, and (2) it interferes with our relationship with him. Guilt says, "I did something wrong."

Shame, on the other hand, is not from God, but rather is the enemy's perversion of godly guilt. Shame says, "I am something wrong." And that is so totally not true. Ever. That's a lie. Shame is a liar.

Shame is the false belief that I am uniquely and fatally flawed. [1]

Lie #1: "I am flawed." There's something wrong with me. I can't let anyone see. I live in the fear that someone somewhere will find out my secret. I'd better keep them at a distance.

Lie #2: "I am uniquely flawed." No one is as bad as me. I am the only one with this problem. If they really knew how bad I am, they would hate me like I hate me.

Lie #3: "I am fatally flawed." I can't be fixed. My flaws are permanent; it's just the way I am. The best I can do is hide them and control the situation (and everyone else) so no one ever finds out.

Shame holds so many people, even Christians, in prison, keeping them from living out their true identity, and even from knowing what it is. Yes, Christians are forgiven, but so often live an unhealed life in shame. This is tragic.

But there's good news.

There is victory over shame. His name is Jesus, and he's made a way.

Shame's power over us is really just a house of cards because it's built on lies. The truth of God's word blows it away.

---

[1] This excellent definition of shame comes from *Restoring the Foundations* ministry: https://RestoringTheFoundations.org

Each of shame's three lies described above get smashed to pieces by the Word of God. We have victory over shame when we choose to replace its lies with God's truth:

- I'm not something wrong (Psalm 139:14).
- I am made in God's own image (Genesis 1:27).
- I am a new creation (2 Corinthians 5:17).
- God loves me apart from what I do (Ephesians 1:4).
- I am not uniquely flawed; I'm not the only one struggling with this (1 Corinthians 10:13).
- I am not fatally flawed. My sin is not bigger or more powerful than Jesus' blood. Jesus' blood is bigger and stronger than any and all of my sin (Isaiah 53:5).

Scripture References

I praise you because I am fearfully and wonderfully made; your works are wonderful, I know that full well. (Psalm 139:14)

God created mankind in his own image, in the image of God he created them; male and female he created them. (Genesis 1:27)

If anyone is in Christ, that person is a new creation: The old has gone, the new is here! (2 Corinthians 5:17)

He chose us in him before the creation of the world to be holy and blameless in his sight. (Ephesians 1:4)

No temptation has overtaken you except what is common to mankind. And God is faithful; he will not let you be tempted beyond what you can bear. But when you are tempted, he will also provide a way out so that you can endure it. (1 Corinthians 10:13)

He was pierced for our transgressions, he was crushed for our iniquities; the punishment that brought us peace was on him, and by his wounds we are healed. (Isaiah 53:5)

That's why Jesus said, "You will know the truth and the truth will set you free" (John 8:32).

Victory over shame opens up a whole new adventure to the life God created us to live and Jesus died to restore.

You can't heal shame by pointing it out.

To steward wounded hearts well, we need to understand shame and learn to recognize it. Because wounded people often feel tremendous, debilitating shame.

But do not point it out!

Remember, shame is doing everything it can to stay hidden. It devours a tremendous amount of a wounded person's energy for this purpose.

"Ok, so why don't we want to expose it then?!?" Because if you do, you convince them the shame was right. When they feel safe enough with you, they'll reveal it.

But if we reveal it before they're ready, we're just piling on more shame. They feel shamed for having shame! All that does is (1) identify you as an unsafe person, not someone they can trust, and (2) drive them deeper underground, getting better at concealing it.

"So if I'm not going to expose their shame, why do I need to learn to recognize it?" Because it's a signal to you that you're dealing with someone who is very wounded. Go slow. Handle them with kid gloves. Be as affirming as you can.

So don't shame them for having shame. Instead, validate the pain they feel. After you've built an affirming, safe relationship, let them reveal what they are ashamed of when they are ready.

Practical takeaways from this chapter:

- Guilt says, "I did something wrong."
- Shame says, "I am something wrong."
- Shame is a belief that "I am uniquely and fatally flawed."
- We need to recognize shame because it's a sign of wounding.
- Build a safe relationship. They will share when they're ready.

Never expose someone's shame; that convinces them shame was right. Instead, build a safe relationship, affirming God's truths that you see in them.

- 42 -

Chapter 5:
Understanding the nature of wounding: Unworthiness & trauma

As my wife Janet and I work with people to facilitate God's healing in their lives, we see a common obstacle that holds many people back. Some people can't even approach God to have a conversation about healing, because of one thing:

Unworthiness.

Wounded people have a deep-seated, underlying feeling of unworthiness and the shame that comes with it.

In my experience, feeling unworthy is one of the hardest obstacles to overcome, because most people don't correctly understand why they feel unworthy. And if they don't even understand why they feel that way, it becomes really hard to address the root of the problem.

But before we unpack that, a caveat first.

Jesus took unworthiness off the table at the cross.

This is when all the Biblical scholars and theologians out there quote me all the Bible verses about our sinful nature, our unworthiness before a holy God, and how we can't save ourselves. Yes and amen. I know all that, and I agree.

I'm taking for granted we all understand that, yes, of course we are all unworthy (Romans 3:10-11). None of us deserve the grace we've been given. None of us deserve a relationship with God. None of us deserve his favor. My point is not to encourage entitlement.

But wasn't our unworthiness the whole point of the cross? Jesus took all our unworthiness and nailed it to the cross, so when God looks at us, he sees Christ's worthiness (2 Corinthians 5:21).

That's not license to presume on God's grace and live however sinfully we want (Romans 6:1-2, Philippians 2:14-16). It's recognition of the fact that, in order to restore relationship with God, Jesus took worthiness off the table at the cross.

So let's talk about why we really feel unworthy. We can't move past the unworthiness that Jesus died for if we don't even understand why we feel it in the first place.

Scripture References

[10] As it is written: "There is no one righteous, not even one; [11] there is no one who understands; there is no one who seeks God." (Romans 3:10-11)

God made him who had no sin to be sin for us, so that in him we might become the righteousness of God. (2 Corinthians 5:21)

[1] What shall we say, then? Shall we go on sinning so that grace may increase? [2] By no means! We are those who have died to sin; how can we live in it any longer? (Romans 6:1-2)

> [14] Do everything without grumbling or arguing, [15] so that you may become blameless and pure, "children of God without fault in a warped and crooked generation." Then you will shine among them like stars in the sky [16] as you hold firmly to the word of life. And then I will be able to boast on the day of Christ that I did not run or labor in vain. (Philippians 2:14-16)

People think they feel unworthy because of what they're ashamed of.

People think they feel unworthy because of that thing they're ashamed of. "I'm so _____." Fill in the blank with the negative adjective for you. Fat? Weak? Stupid? Vulgar? Dirty? (Feeling dirty is common for people who have been abused.) Or maybe sinful? Or angry? Broken? Not good enough? Flawed? Defective?

What do our thoughts constantly accuse us of? What do you, deep down in your heart, accuse yourself of?

The truth is, those are lies people believe. Sorting out lies is tricky. The nature of being deceived is that we don't know we're deceived. It's hard to identify the lies someone believes so deeply that they just take them for granted.

But even if those things were true, which they aren't, it still wouldn't matter. Those things are irrelevant because that's not how God sees the person. That's not how God sees us.

People really feel unworthy because of wounding.

The truth is, Jesus nailed all that negative stuff, both from our past and what we're struggling with now, to the cross. And, honestly, none of that is why people feel unworthy (although that's why they think they feel unworthy).

So here's the paradigm shift:

People feel unworthy because they're wounded. That's what wounding does. It makes you feel unworthy. And often, yes, it uses shame to do that. But the underlying problem is the wounding, not the shame.

Feeling shame, feeling unworthy, is a sign that they have broken places in their heart that God wants to heal. That's why the last chapter focused on understanding and recognizing shame. Because it's a sign of wounding. And God wants to heal it.

Now let's understand some basics about the nature of wounding.

How to understand wounding, trauma, and the language of the heart.

In order to steward wounded hearts well, we need to understand two types of trauma. [1] What we normally think of as trauma is Type "B" Trauma, Bad Thing Happened.

---

[1] This book is not intended to be a thorough education on trauma, so I'm not going into simple vs. complex trauma here. Although useful to understand, that is out-of-scope for this book. For a more detailed explanation of trauma, see the book *Complex PTSD: From Surviving to Thriving: A Guide and Map for Recovering from Childhood Trauma* by Pete Walker.

But there's another kind of trauma that can be just as damaging: When the necessary good thing fails to happen. We call that Type "A" Trauma, the Absence of the Necessary Good Thing. Both types of trauma can be just as damaging.

Typically, the trauma in a person's life is not their fault. Yes, as sinful humans living in a fallen world, we are perfectly capable of inflicting trauma upon ourselves.

But in most cases the initial trauma is not the person's fault.

For example, yes, the trauma caused in a person's life by an addiction (gambling, alcohol, drugs, sex, etc.) is their fault. But usually, they're using that addiction to medicate pain from an earlier trauma that is rarely their fault; for example, abuse (Type B trauma) or abandonment (Type A trauma).

Another example: I think we'd agree that if someone crashes their car driving 100 mph, the physical trauma they incur is their fault. I would argue the real problem is, What lie do they believe that convinced them driving so recklessly was a good idea?

Even when someone's trauma is caused by their own foolish behavior, you have to get to the root of why the foolish behavior was there in the first place. And often that's hidden below the surface.

So even if, as is usually the case, the trauma someone experiences is not their fault, their response to it is.

Because of what happened, or what failed to happen, what judgements did they make about themselves? About God? About other people? About the world? About how they would be treated?

Based on their judgments of themselves, God, other people, and the world, how did they vow to protect their heart?

We make these vows because we're trying to protect our heart ourselves instead of trusting God.

An Example of Type "A" Trauma

Here's an example of Type "A" Trauma, the Absence of the Necessary Good Thing.

Suppose a parent was physically present but emotionally absent. If it's your mother, maybe you were never emotionally nurtured. You never learned you could be loved just for yourself.

If it's your father, maybe you were never affirmed and approved, never called into who God created you to be, never given permission to be your true self. You only were acceptable if you performed properly.

Either way, what might you have judged about yourself, God, other people, and the world? Maybe one of these:

- *"I'm not worthy of love in and of myself."*
- *"I'm only loved if I perform."*
- *"No one will love me for me."*

- *"If I don't give people a reason to love me, they won't."*
- *"People will only love me if there's something in it for them."*

Because of that, what might you vow to protect your heart? Maybe one of these:

- *"I will always be the good person to earn love."*
- *"I will never disappoint anyone."*
- *"I will never let anyone come close enough to see the real me."*
- *"I will reject others before they can reject me."*

So if a person vows, *"I'll always be a good person and never disappoint anyone,"* can you see how they could have trouble setting boundaries and saying no? Do you see how that vow sets them up for relationships with toxic controllers, those who are looking for just such people to take advantage of?

Can you see how this person might find themselves struggling with, *"Why am I always so exhausted and unfulfilled when I'm doing so many good things?"*

Or suppose a person vows, *"I'll never let anyone close enough to see the real me because then they will stop loving me. I'll reject them before they can reject me."* Can you see how this sets them up for failure in their relationships? They sabotage themselves by (1) quitting relationships with healthy people who want intimacy, and (2) pursuing relationships with toxic people who don't require intimacy.

Can you see how these deep inner beliefs and vows we take for granted wreak havoc in our lives?

Often people make these inner vows in their spirits at a very young age, even as a baby or toddler before learning language, which makes them very hard to discover and articulate. So we need the Holy Spirit's help in discovering them.

Inner healing isn't about digging stuff up from the past or blaming parents. But if past woundings are causing bad fruit in life today, those woundings aren't in the past at all, are they? They are very much here in the present, causing damage that God wants to heal.

God isn't looking for worthiness. He's looking for willingness.

Jesus took worthiness off the table at the cross. God isn't looking for worthiness. He's looking for willingness.

Healing requires the willingness to expose, to a loving God and in a safe space, those scary places that have been buried for a long time. Not to relive the trauma. But so that God can heal it.

Like life-saving surgery, healing wounding hurts. And there's a recovery period. Just like physical therapy after a surgery, people may need spiritual and/or emotional therapy for a while after receiving inner healing.

But getting their life back is worth it.

Practical takeaways from this chapter:

- Jesus took worthiness off the table at the cross.
- People feel unworthy because they're wounded.
- Type "A" trauma (the "Absence" of the necessary good thing) can be just as devastating as Type "B" trauma ("Bad" thing happened).
- God isn't looking for worthiness. He's looking for willingness.

Don't shame people for feeling unworthy, or let them shame themselves. Be a safe place where they can share their wounding. Because that's the first step to healing.

- 52 -

Chapter 6:
Don't push wounded people into cheap forgiveness.

Cheap forgiveness is worse than none.

We can unknowingly do tremendous damage if we push or guilt people into forgiving too soon.

What?!? The Bible commands us to forgive! Nothing derails a person's healing faster than unforgiveness!

Yes, totally true. I completely believe in the power of forgiveness, no argument there. But it has to be real forgiveness.

Forgiveness is one of the most misunderstood topics today, both by our culture and by the Church. True forgiveness is not an event. It's not something you help someone do at 3:07 PM on Tuesday. In fact, it's not something you help them *do* at all. It is a process you *walk with them through.*

In our zeal, we often push wounded people into forgiving too soon, before they're ready. If we pressure them into forgiveness before they've done the work to come to a place of real forgiveness, then we've just had them check a box of cheap forgiveness.

Cheap forgiveness is worse than none. Because they think they've forgiven, but they really haven't. So we unknowingly lead them into living in unforgiveness with all its negative consequences.

10 things forgiveness is not.

Sometimes it's easier to understand what something is by understanding what it's not. Here are ten things forgiveness is not that people often mistake for forgiveness.

Forgiveness is NOT:

1. Pretending nothing happened.
2. Covering for the other person.
3. Trusting someone who should not be trusted.
4. Giving a perpetrator access so they can do it again.
5. Lacking healthy boundaries.
6. Letting a criminal go free.
7. Avoiding conflict.
8. Pretending to agree with the other person when you really don't.
9. Feeling happy about something bad that happened.
10. An emotion or a feeling at all.

Forgiveness and healing are two different things (Gun Range Parable).

Say we go to the gun range together. I'm handling my weapon carelessly and accidentally shoot you in the shoulder. You can forgive me instantly, but a gunshot wound takes time to heal.

Suppose I see you the next day after you're released from the hospital. I slap you on the shoulder, "Hey, how are you doing? Great to see you! Sorry again about yesterday."

"Ouch!" you respond, because I slapped your shoulder right on the wound. "That hurts!"

"Why are you still hurting? Haven't you forgiven me?" I ask indignantly. "What's wrong with you? You're not a very good Christian! You're being very unforgiving."

But forgiveness has nothing to do with it! You forgave me on the way to the hospital, but you still have the wound. There's nothing wrong with you; it's normal for you to hurt again if I slap the wound. My refusal to acknowledge the reality of the wound I've given you is really a sign of my own spiritual immaturity and lack of repentance.

Forgiveness just means we don't hold anything against the person; it doesn't mean we're instantly healed from the wounding they caused.

Setting healthy boundaries is not unforgiveness.

We often hear, "I can't forgive that person; they'll just do it again," as if forgiveness means they have to pretend it never happened, giving an abuser full access to continue their abuse.

In fact, it's common for abusive narcissists to prey on this misunderstanding of forgiveness. *"Aren't you a Christian? You're supposed to forgive me! I said I was sorry!"*

Forgiveness doesn't mean a person can't set healthy boundaries. Forgiveness also doesn't mean they have to place themselves at risk with an unhealthy person.

With an unhealthy or toxic person, their words don't matter. Talk is cheap. It's only what they do that actually matters.

In the gunshot example, if I've made no change in my behavior and I'm still handling my weapon carelessly, it's perfectly reasonable for you to put up a boundary and not go to the gun range with me until I get some safety training. That's not unforgiveness. That's wisdom.

Another example: Many churches have done damage to battered wives by counseling them to just forget the abuse they endured in the name of "forgiveness." After all, their husband said he was sorry. (See "Examples of Healthy Boundaries in Domestic Violence" on the next page.)

In a relationship, we are trusting the other person to protect our heart. If they instead betray and abuse it, we can set boundaries to protect our heart. Boundaries are a pullback from intimacy. Sometimes they can be temporary, sometimes permanent. It depends if the other person is willing to do their work in the relationship.

Examples of Healthy Boundaries in Domestic Violence

Although a bit off-topic, I'm including this because Christians often do not understand healthy boundaries around abuse. Abuse victims, especially battered wives, are some of the most wounded hearts we have grievously not stewarded well. This has to change.

While this greatly over-simplifies the issue, here are some examples of healthy boundaries around domestic violence.

- Law enforcement is called in, and he is arrested for assault.

- He's kicked out of the house. The church helps her find community resources to cover budgetary shortfalls.

- If she lets him back in the house at all, which she does not have to do, it's only after at least 12 months of him getting consistent counseling. Faithfully; no missed appointments, no starting-and-stopping games.

- When narcissists want the appearance of changing without really changing, they go to counseling just long enough to make it appear like they are serious about it. But then some excuse derails them, and they start missing sessions. None of that nonsense should be tolerated.

- He has to prove to her satisfaction that he's done his own work.

- In parallel with all of that, the pastor recommends a good trauma therapist for her, and maybe the church pays for it. Her close friends (not everyone) know what happened and support her working through it over time.

- A great resource for domestic violence is the National Domestic Violence Hotline at 800-799-7233.

- I highly recommend the book "*It Is Abuse?*" by Darby A. Strickland for helpers and clergy wanting to learn more about the practical side of recognizing abuse and helping victims.

Forgiveness is a one-way transaction between the wounded party and God. Restoring a relationship through reconciliation is a two-way transaction and depends on the other person's willingness to repent and change.

Putting up a boundary to prevent further wounding does not mean the wounded person hasn't forgiven.

Minimizing sin is not forgiveness.

We see people stuck in denial all the time. You can tell because they minimize the sin against them, making excuses for the other person: "it wasn't that bad" or "they didn't mean it" or "they were going through a really hard time."

I'm not talking about things people do accidentally. I'm talking about the big stuff. I'm talking about when the sin really was that bad, and yes, they did mean it.

Covering for the other person is not forgiveness. Downplaying how bad it was is not forgiveness. It's actually dishonoring to the other person to minimize their bad behavior. Doing so keeps them from the help they might otherwise receive if the truth comes out.

Minimizing the sin actually harms the person who committed it. Downplaying the sin is actually lying about how bad it was. Although it appears to be honoring, lying never brings honor, because it allows evil to continue unchecked in the other person. And that's not love.

Also, minimizing the sin harms the wounded person. Downplaying the other person's sin against them is actually unforgiveness. Pretending the wrong wasn't wrong actually hinders forgiveness. If it wasn't so bad then there's nothing to forgive, is there?

For example, suppose their dad was abusive. Trying to forgive, they minimize the sin by saying, "He sometimes got a little angry. But only when we were disobedient and deserved it. It wasn't that bad." Encouraging this leads them into cheap forgiveness.

By pretending it was ok, when it was far from ok, we lead the wounded person to live in unforgiveness. They forgive a small sin, a sin that "wasn't that bad." But they've not forgiven the real sin, the sin that, yes, really was that bad. So they are still living in unforgiveness toward the real sin committed against them. (More about this in the next chapter.)

Forgiveness is not pretending the other person did not do evil. Forgiveness is coming to the place where the other person is not defined by the evil they did.

Forgiveness does not mean a wounded person has to publicly share their story.

Their story is their story. It belongs to them. They can choose to share it or not. Never pressure someone into sharing their story. Sharing it is a precious gift that deserves to be stewarded well by the hearers.

They get to decide if they feel safe sharing their story. Or if they even want to. It's between them and God; stay out of it.

Unfortunately, some Christian leaders are not above using a person's story to build their own empire. Here are some ways leaders can nicely, but manipulatively, coerce a wounded person into sharing their "testimony" for the leader's benefit:

- **Shame:** *"If you're not ready to share your testimony, you must not be healed yet."*

- **Manipulation:** *"You have a responsibility to share your testimony. Look at how many people it would help."*

- **Presumption:** Assuming that you're going to share, without asking you, and informing you of when you're on the calendar.

- **Comparison:** *"Everyone else (or so-and-so) is sharing their story."*

None of these tactics are from God. Doing any of these things is a sign that the leader is steamrolling over the hearts of wounded people to build their own empire.

Don't do more damage by pushing them into forgiveness before they are ready.

Practical takeaways from this chapter:

- Don't confuse not yet being healed from wounding with unforgiveness.
- Don't confuse setting healthy boundaries with unforgiveness.
- Help people articulate how bad the sin against them really was.
- Never push anyone to share their story or testimony.

Don't push people into cheap forgiveness, which is worse than none. It leaves them (unknowingly) living in unforgiveness.

Chapter 7:
Real forgiveness is grief work.

So how do we walk with a wounded person through real forgiveness? *What is real forgiveness anyway?* I'm glad you asked! Here we go.

7 things forgiveness is.

Forgiveness IS:

1. An act of the will (versus an emotion).
2. A process that takes time.
3. A decision to begin the process.
4. Releasing what we hold against the other person.
5. Canceling the bill they owe us.
6. Grieving the loss caused by the sin against us.
7. Coming to the place where the other person is not defined by the evil they did to us.

Forgiveness is a process, not an event.

The sin against a person is a loss in that person's life. Forgiveness is the process of grieving that loss.

The process of forgiveness parallels the process of grief. You may be familiar with the 5 phases of grief:

- Denial

- Anger

- Bargaining

- Depression or Sadness

- Acceptance

These phases aren't numbered because they don't necessarily go in order, and they often repeat. They are all healthy and necessary for a season. The trick is not to get stuck in one of them for too long. How long is "too long"? There's no formula; it subjectively depends on the situation and the person doing the grieving.

Forgiveness works the same way because real forgiveness is grieving a loss. Maybe of innocence. Maybe of dreams. Maybe of trust. Maybe of a relationship that wasn't what the person thought it was. Maybe they came to the painful realization that a relationship will never be the good thing it could be because the other person refuses to do their own work.

Real forgiveness is grieving a loss.

The thing is, to truly forgive, they have to grieve the loss. It's a process, not an event.

No one walks up to a widow after her husband's funeral and says, "Well, that was a great service. I'm so glad for you that you're done grieving now."

We all understand that grieving is a process, not an event. We all understand that the widow's grieving process is just beginning, and we'd all expect it to take several years. [1] We'd all expect her to bounce between days like these:

- *"I can't believe he's really gone."*

- *"I'm angry that he's gone. It's just not fair."*

- *"I'm sad that he's gone. I miss him so much my heart is breaking."*

- *"Today was a good day."*

Her friends aren't concerned if she has an angry day or a depressed week, or if they see her in any of the other phases of grief. They become concerned, however, if she is stuck in one of the phases for months or years on end. Going through the phases of grief is not a problem. Getting stuck in one of them is.

Forgiveness is the same way. *"I said a prayer of forgiveness for that person who abused me. I'm glad that's over and done with."* Unfortunately, it doesn't work that way. Forgiveness is a process, not an event. Going through the phases of forgiveness is not a problem. Getting stuck in one of them is.

---

[1] It takes the average person three years to grieve the loss of a loved one (from the book *Recovering from the Losses of Life* by Norman Wright).

While the widow's friends would understand her needing more alone time than usual, they'd rightfully worry if she pulled away from them completely.

Wise friends let the widow know they respect her process. They let her know they can be as close or as far as she needs them to be on any given day. They're ok with giving her space or being with her.

And they don't try to push her through the other phases of grief before she's ready. It has to be on her timeline, or she won't receive the healing her heart needs from the grieving process.

We can walk with wounded people through the phases of forgiveness the same way.

A person can't forgive until they've gotten angry. Don't talk them out of their anger.

A common thing we hear is, "I can't forgive them, I'm still angry about it." Good! Actually, being angry about the evil done to them is a healthy part of forgiveness. Just like anger is one of the phases of grief, it is a legitimate phase of the forgiveness process.

They can't forgive what they don't acknowledge as wrong. If something heinous was done to them, they should be angry about it!

Anger is a key ingredient, and often the first step, to real forgiveness. I know that's counter-intuitive, but stay with me here.

I'm talking about the really bad stuff. I'm not talking about getting cut off in traffic or losing a parking space. Hopefully we can all forgive petty things without needing to get angry. But to forgive the big stuff—abuse, abandonment, rejection, neglect, manipulation, betrayal, rape, coercion into an abortion—the person has to get angry first. For a season.

Anger is actually a good thing. The truth is God made anger. He gave us the potential for that emotion. And used correctly, it's a good and necessary thing.

Ephesians 4:26-27

[26] In your anger do not sin. Do not let the sun go down while you are still angry, [27] and do not give the devil a foothold.

God doesn't say to never be angry. But he shows us how to steward it rightly. "Do not let the sun go down while you are still angry" doesn't literally mean you have to complete the forgiveness process by bedtime. It means give your anger a short season.

Staying in anger too long gives the devil a foothold as our righteous anger can morph into bitterness. In the Church, we've often misinterpreted this to mean, "Never get angry because anger is bad." Not true.

Anger is a godly response to injustice. What we consider unjust displays our spiritual maturity, but we should all be angry over a true injustice. That's not wrong; that's godly.

If someone has committed a serious injustice, the wounded person should be angry. In fact, they can't come to a place of forgiveness unless they get angry. It's part of the forgiveness process. Here's why.

There's no reason to forgive something that wasn't a sin. *"It wasn't that bad,"* is a phrase we commonly hear from trauma victims.

Unless they get as angry as the sin was heinous, they're minimizing the sin against them. For example, if they were abused, coerced, raped, lied to, manipulated, don't minimize the sin against them, or let them downplay it. Like we talked about in the last chapter, yes, it really was that bad.

By "get angry," we're not talking about justifying an unhealthy expression of anger, like rage or revenge. We're talking about encouraging them to be honest about the anger they truly feel, naming it for what it is.

Until they acknowledge their anger, they're forgiving the wrong sin. Like we talked about in the last chapter, they're not forgiving the real sin against them. They're forgiving some other sin that "wasn't that bad." And if they aren't forgiving the real sin, they're actually living in unforgiveness.

Expanding the "abusive parent" example from the last chapter, suppose that as a child they didn't clean their room when they were told to. And their parent severely beat them in a drunken rage. Looking back on it years later, they say, "Yeah it was a little over the top, but I deserved it. I should've cleaned my room." So they forgive a small sin, discipline that was "a little over the top."

But that was not the real sin against them. The real sin against them was abuse, a severe beating that no child deserves. It was also neglect; as their caregiver, their parent never should've been drunk in the first place.

So it was not "a little over the top." It was cruel and terrible. They were horribly treated. It was as wrong as wrong could be. It was abuse and neglect against a child the parent should've been caring for. Those are the sins they need to forgive. And the full realization of that should make them angry.

It's important for them to acknowledge the full extent of the sin against them. It should make them angry. It's only from that place they can bring their anger to the cross and let it all out. Upon expressing it, they can let Jesus have it.

It's only by acknowledging how much they are owed that they can truly forgive, coming to the place where the perpetrator doesn't owe them anything. It's only by acknowledging the full extent of the debt that they can forgive the debt.

No one wants to get stuck in anger. Some people do, and their unforgiveness tears them up. But it's important that they get angry for a season. Don't talk them out of it.

Don't shame them out of it. Let them sit in it for a bit; that is a healthy part of their healing.

Do you discern that a wounded person needs to forgive? Don't force, guilt, shame, or manipulate them into forgiveness before they're ready. Instead, help them grieve their loss. Forgiveness will come in time, when their grief moves into the acceptance phase.

Practical takeaways from this chapter:

- Forgiveness is a process, not an event.

- Real forgiveness is grieving a loss.

- A person can't forgive (the really bad stuff) until they've gotten angry about the actual sin against them.

- Until they acknowledge the gravity of the sin against them, they are forgiving the wrong sin. Then they live in unforgiveness with regard to the actual sin done against them.

The best way to help someone forgive is to walk with them through grieving the loss. Because real forgiveness is grief work.

Chapter 8:
We blame trauma survivors to make our world feel safe. So do they.

It's wrong to blame trauma survivors for something that wasn't their fault.

We have a nasty habit of blaming trauma survivors for the trauma they endured, trauma perpetrated upon them through no fault of their own. Often, we don't realize we're doing it, because we simultaneously feel compassion for them.

Yes, unwise choices can put people in a situation where trauma is more likely to happen. But no one deserves trauma, ever, regardless of what unwise choices they may have made.

How many times have you heard something like this:

"Dressing like that, she's just asking to be raped." No. A thousand times no. No woman deserves to be raped. Ever. I've been shocked to hear Christian brothers say this. Something this vile should never come out of the mouth of a Christian man.

"She must not have been very attentive at home," when blaming a wife for her husband's affair. I've actually most often heard this from other Christian women. No. No spouse ever deserves to be cheated on, no matter what the situation is. A person's adultery is no one's fault but his (or her) own. Ever.

"They must not have been good parents," when blaming the people down the street for their teen's suicide. No. Never. No parent ever deserves to bury their child, whether through intentional or accidental tragedy.

And saddest of all, childhood trauma survivors blame themselves. *"It's my fault my father (or mother or sibling) sexually abused me. There's something wrong with me."* No. Never true. Yet this response is common.

The lie of "it's their fault" is safer to believe than the truth of an unsafe world.

Why do we blame trauma survivors? Why do trauma survivors blame themselves?

While it's counter-intuitive, there's actually a very logical reason: It's the safest conclusion. [1]

Which is safer for a victim of childhood trauma to believe?

- The lie: "There's something wrong with me. It's my fault this happened."

- The truth: "I am in the care of a monster. There is something seriously wrong with my dad (or my mom)."

The lie is actually the safer conclusion! "If it's my fault, then maybe I have some control over it. If I can just be a better daughter (or son), this won't happen again."

---

[1] Credit to Dr. Gabor Mate, author of the book *In the Realm of Hungry Ghosts*, for drawing this conclusion.

Believing the truth, "I'm in the care of a monster. I've got no control over when this happens again," makes the world a very scary, unsafe place. The lie is actually a psychological defense mechanism used by children so they can survive.

Take the woman whose friend's husband had an affair. Which is safer to believe?

- The lie: "If she'd just been a better wife, he wouldn't have cheated on her."
- The truth: "His affair was not her fault. He made his own choice."

Or take the example of parents you know whose teen was lost to suicide. Which is safer to believe?

- The lie: "They must be bad parents. That would never happen in my house."
- The truth: "What a horrible thing to happen to them. No parents deserve to go through that."

In each case, the lie is a "safer" conclusion to believe. Believing the lie that trauma is the fault of the survivors gives us a feeling of control over our unsafe world.

- "If I'm a good wife, my husband won't cheat on me."
- "If we're good parents, our children will be safe."

The problem is, it's only a false feeling of control. We really have very little, if any, control over the unsafe, fallen world we live in.

Our only true security in this unsafe world is in the goodness of God.

The truth is, in this unsafe world, our safety is out of our control. The only true security we really have is in the goodness of God. Yet even Jesus did not promise us safety; in fact, he promised the opposite.

John 16:33

"In this world you will have trouble. But take heart! I have overcome the world." – Jesus

God's security is not the absence of trauma or tragedy in this life. But Jesus promises to be with us as we walk through it.

Don't try to pull someone out of the pain.
Walk with them through it.

As Christians, we should follow Jesus' example, and be with each other through trauma and the pain of this life.

Psalm 23:4

Even though I walk through the valley of the shadow of death, I will fear no evil, for you are with me; your rod and your staff, they comfort me.

When people are going through the Valley of the Shadow of Death, don't try to find them an off-ramp. Yes, it's natural to want to pull someone out of the Valley of the Shadow of Death. We mean well. But we can't pull them out of it. Jesus is calling us to walk with them through it.

Job's friends get a bad rap most of the time, which is well deserved. They blamed him for his trauma and did not steward his heart well.

But when they first showed up on the scene, they got it right for a whole week when they just sat there with Job, in silence, in the ashes of his life.

Job 2:11-13

11 When Job's three friends, Eliphaz the Temanite, Bildad the Shuhite and Zophar the Naamathite, heard about all the troubles that had come upon him, they set out from their homes and met together by agreement to go and sympathize with him and comfort him. 12 When they saw him from a distance, they could hardly recognize him; they began to weep aloud, and they tore their robes and sprinkled dust on their heads. 13 Then they sat on the ground with him for seven days and seven nights. No one said a word to him, because they saw how great his suffering was.

Then they opened their mouths, and it was all downhill from there! The rest of the book of Job is basically Job's friends blaming him for his trauma. "C'mon, Job, come clean! What did you do to deserve this? You know this is all your fault!"

And Job saying over and over again, "No, guys, it's really not!"

We must stop blaming trauma survivors, and help them to not blame themselves. The world is not a safe place. We need to accept that, yes, it could happen to us too. But God is good, even if it does.

As Jesus' hands, feet, mouth, and heart to a wounded world, we have to get this right. As we learn to be Jesus to the hurting, we teach them to be Jesus to us. After all, no one gets out of this world unscathed.

Practical takeaways from this chapter:

- We blame trauma survivors for their trauma so we can believe our world is safe.

- Trauma survivors blame themselves for the same reason.

- Our world is not safe. Our only true security is in the goodness of God, even in the middle of hard things.

- Don't try to pull someone out of the pain. Walk with them through it.

Don't blame trauma survivors for their trauma. Instead, by not judging people for what's happened to them, we make the Church a safe place to make their wounding known.

Stewarding Wounded Hearts

Chapter 9:
Don't practice Christian peer pressure. Honor their no and their process.

Peer pressure. We condemn it in our children when we see it on the playground. In fact, much of our effort in guiding our school age children revolves around teaching them how to not succumb to peer pressure. We know it's not a good thing.

But far too often we do it to each other in church. Not intentionally. We don't realize we're doing it. But we quite often are. And it does a lot of damage to wounded hearts inside a church.

No, there's not really peer pressure in the church, is there?

Yes, there is peer pressure in the church.

Yes, unfortunately, there is Christian peer pressure in the church. It actually looks good on the surface, but it is really ugly. It is not the Kingdom of God. Here are three examples.

Example 1: Someone else is expressing their Christianity differently in a way we don't understand. So we punish them. Nasty glares. Avoidance. Gossip. Judgmental thoughts that sneak out on our faces. Looking the other way when passing them in the hallway.

In one church setting, it might look like, "How dare they lift their hands during worship!" In another church setting, it might look like, "How dare they not lift their hands during worship!"

(Aside: And to both the Holy Spirit says, "Why are you looking at the other person during worship instead of Jesus?")

Example 2: A young mother, just saved, admits to her women's Bible study group that she's having a tough time. She admits to having an abortion years ago, and since getting saved, is grieving for her lost child. The older women scowl at her and say, "Don't you know that everything in your past is under the Blood? If you're not full of the joy of the Lord, are you even saved?"

(Aside: There's a mile of difference between being forgiven and being healed. If you're post-abortive and grieving, that's a sign this is your season of healing. [1]*)*

Example 3: A pastor or worship leader works up the emotion during worship. "Come on, church! Let's worship Jesus, he's worthy! Sing louder! Sing with me!"

(Aside: Yes, he is worthy, but you can't force or manipulate worship out of people. You can force and manipulate singing, dancing and carrying on, but worship has to be given freely or it's not worship.)

---

[1] Here are some resources that provide post-abortive healing:
Rachel's Vineyard: https://www.RachelsVineyard.org
Support After Abortion: https://SupportAfterAbortion.com
Project Rachel: https://HopeAfterAbortion.com

Christian Peer Pressure is NOT ok.
God honors our choices.

We try to force other people to stay within the experience we're comfortable with. Christian peer pressure says, *"Conform! You're only a good Christian if you fit into this mold. Be comfortable in there, and don't be peeking out over the edge!"*

To be sure, there are some non-negotiables in Christianity:

- Jesus is the name above every name and the only path to God.

- In fact, Jesus is God. (That whole Trinity thing: Father, Son and Holy Spirit.)

- He's the God who loved us enough to become human and die for us when we hated him. Jesus was the only person ever who was born to die. All to demonstrate his love for us. What kind of over-the-top, wild, passionate love does that? Crazy stuff.

- And there are a few others I won't go into here for lack of space. But you know them: Fruit of the Spirit. Giving. Respect. Sexual integrity. Etc.

But here's the deal. God is anti-peer pressure. God doesn't force us or manipulate us into his way of living. He gives us a choice. In fact, he's so into this that there's a whole book of the Bible, Deuteronomy, dedicated to nothing but

God articulating our choice so we can make an informed decision.

Deuteronomy 30:19b-20a

[19b] I have set before you life and death, blessings and curses. Now choose life, so that you and your children may live [20a] and that you may love the Lord your God, listen to his voice, and hold fast to him.

It's the same choice today as he gave the children of Israel as they were about to enter the Promised Land. But it's our choice. If we don't choose God's ways, it breaks his heart. He weeps for us and for the pain we're bringing on ourselves. But God honors our choice by giving us over to the logical consequences of it.

Peer pressure is never healthy, even if it's for a good thing.

Many people have told me about how they've made beneficial changes in their life as a result of "positive" peer pressure. I don't want to discount anyone's story. I believe them.

But just because the result was positive doesn't mean the method was healthy. God can use even our unhealthy methods to bring about his goals. (Romans 8:28)

Wouldn't a healthy community exert positive, non-judgmental, peer pressure?

> **Romans 8:28**
>
> We know that in all things God works for the good of those who love him, who have been called according to his purpose.

No. I'm picking a fight with the phrase "peer pressure." Peer pressure is never healthy, because it's based on pressure. God doesn't pressure. He invites. He honors our choice by giving us the consequences we choose, for good or ill.

So I would redefine *positive, non-judgmental, peer pressure* as *exhortation*.

Exhortation means to "strongly encourage or urge." [1] It is the art of telling someone a truth they don't necessarily want to hear, but need to hear. Exhortation has its place.

But it gets tricky, because it's easy to confuse godly exhortation with Christian peer pressure.

The difference, though, is that after giving someone a godly exhortation, we honor their choice. They have the right to not take our advice. We don't punish them if they reject what we have to say.

Exhortation affirms who the person really is in Christ and invites them to step into their heavenly identity. Peer pressure threatens to shame them if they don't comply. Do you see the difference?

---

[1] According to Google's Generative AI, searching for "biblical meaning of exhortation." https://www.google.com/search?q=biblical+meaning+of+exhortation, accessed 4/27/2024.

Don't be afraid of people's bad choices.

When we become afraid of people's bad choices, it's easy to slip into the subtle manipulation of Christian peer pressure.

But this mistakenly moves the church into the business of sin management instead of transformation. We get more concerned about whether or not people fit the mold, whether or not they're checking all the right external boxes correctly, than we are about the state of their heart.

Sin management is concerned about outward appearances, the visible good or bad fruit in someone's life. Transformation is concerned with healing the bitter roots inside their heart that are causing the bad fruit.

Jesus (and the Bible) Focuses on the Heart

[19] Out of the heart come evil thoughts—murder, adultery, sexual immorality, theft, false testimony, slander. [20a] These are what defile a person. (Matthew 15:19-20a)

A good man brings good things out of the good stored up in his heart, and an evil man brings evil things out of the evil stored up in his heart. For the mouth speaks what the heart is full of. (Luke 6:45)

Above all else, guard your heart, for everything you do flows from it. (Proverbs 4:23)

Yes, behavior matters. But Jesus was always concerned first about the heart. Because the truth is that we can have all the good behavior and still have a heart far from God. But once we get our heart healed, the good behavior (good fruit) always follows.

Remember the problem is not so much a person's sinful lifestyle as the wounding that lifestyle is medicating. And that wounding, at least initially, was almost never their fault.

You don't have to endure people's bad choices.

I'm not saying we should pretend to agree with people's bad choices. The culture is trying to bully us into doing just that, calling us "haters" if we have the audacity to say sinful choices are self-destructive. (That's worldly peer pressure, by the way, and sadly whole denominations have succumbed to it.)

But the truth is not every choice that disagrees with our precious advice is necessarily a bad choice. It might just be different than how we would've done it.

Kind controllers are still unhealthy.

Normally when we think of controlling people, we think of mean, raging T-Rexes. Someone who screams and throws a temper tantrum until they get their way. Maybe they're even physically abusive.

But kind controllers are just as unhealthy.

Have you ever met "can-you-just" people? They are typically very sweet and kind. They can appear very loving. But they don't take no for an answer, which is the definition of a controlling person.

Maybe they ask you to help with Vacation Bible School. You've already got a full plate and can't take on another commitment. So when you say, "No, I'm sorry, I'm really swamped," they respond:

- *"Ok, but can you just bring snacks each day?"*
- *"Ok, but can you just help me with crafts for two hours in the afternoon?"*
- *"Ok, but can you just help me decorate the hallways this Saturday?"*

Very sweetly, kindly, and with a loving, gentle tone of voice, they disrespect your no. *"Ok, but can you just…"* And far too often, we get guilted into doing something we're not called to do, and that distracts us from what we are called to do.

(Aside: The truth is, you do not have to justify, defend, or explain your no. Just keep repeating the word no. Walk away if you have to.)

Often, as we've seen, wounded people are carrying a lot of shame. It's easy for them to fall victim to kind controllers. They are trying so hard, doing "all the things" out of atonement, from a place of shame, rather than from a place of calling.

When we don't honor people's no, we reinforce their wounding.

Too often in a person's story, especially if their story involves abuse, their no was not even heard, let alone honored. So when we don't honor their no, when we say, *"Ok, but can you just …?"* we reinforce the message from their abuse:

- *"You don't have a voice."*
- *"Your preferences don't matter because you don't matter."*
- *"You're only here to serve everyone else. You're second class. You're less than."*

Jesus begs to differ. No one is second class. No one is less than. Everyone's voice matters. The ground is level at the foot of the Cross.

Suppose your church has a phenomenal addiction recovery program. You've heard the testimonies of people who received tremendous freedom from drugs, alcohol, porn, and other forms of addiction.

Someone confides in you that they struggle with alcoholism, and you recommend the program. It's a great program. It really would bring them freedom.

But they say, "Thanks but no thanks." You know this isn't going to end well. But rather than peer pressure them to do the wise thing, you honor their no. They may need to sit in the consequences a bit longer before they're ready.

What you don't know is their story is a story of repeated abuse, where no one has respected their no. That's the pain they're medicating with the alcohol. If you peer pressure them into doing the program, you become just one more voice of coercion.

They know they should do the program. And they expect you to peer pressure them into it. So when you don't, when you honor their no, they don't show it, but they're shocked. It takes them a while to process it. They are feeling honored like they never have before. Because someone, finally, respected their no.

That, in and of itself, is so tremendously healing. You just qualified yourself as a safe person. You don't realize it, but you've just given them a respect and a dignity that no one else ever has. So when the Holy Spirit has moved them into a place where they are ripe for healing, they will likely come back to you and ask for help.

And as they process, they realize that if they want the freedom from their addiction that your church's program offers, you're not going to bully, coerce, guilt, or peer pressure them into it. They are going to have to choose it themselves.

By honoring their no, you've empowered them to make positive choices toward health and healing. Although it may take a little longer, that bodes a much more successful outcome than if you had forced them into it with "positive" Christian peer pressure.

The Kingdom of God is invitational, not controlling.

God never forces us into his calling or his healing. He invites. Peer pressure and control are weapons of the enemy.

At the end of the day, peer pressure, however kind or "positive," is really just bullying. The people of God deserve better.

Never pressure, manipulate, or guilt someone into a ministry, either as a volunteer or as a participant. Wounded people are very vulnerable to this, because of a strong desire to atone, desperately trying to make amends for the shame they carry.

Practical takeaways from this chapter:

- Christian peer pressure is never healthy, even when for a good thing.
- The Church should be about transformation, not sin management.
- Kind controllers are still unhealthy.
- Honor people's no.
- The Kingdom of God is invitational. It is not controlling.

Don't practice Christian peer pressure. Do what our Heavenly Father does: Invite them, but respect their no. Because we don't want to be one more voice of coercion.

Chapter 10:
The Church is a lifesaving station, not a live stage show.

Have we, the people of God, forgotten who we are? Have we forgotten what we're for as God's hands, feet, voice, and heart in the world?

The Lighthouse Parable

Another quiet night's sleep was shattered by the midnight alarm. The claxon sounded in the small, New England lighthouse on the rocky Massachusetts coast. Another ship had run aground on the rocks in the night fog. The men and women in the small, dingy lighthouse jumped out of bed, pulled on their gear, and got to work rescuing the survivors.

The small under-funded dingy building housed a team that "lived the sea." They didn't just "live by the sea." They "lived the sea," just like a sports addict might "live" football. Everything in their life revolved around the sea. The sea was all they talked about. Every activity had something to do with the sea. The sea was their whole life.

They couldn't save everyone from every shipwreck that happened on their watch, but they saved many. It was hard, thankless work, but they loved it. They were sold out for the mission of saving lives from boats wrecked on the rocks in the fog.

One day, the people from the nearby towns who had been saved from drowning by this valiant little lighthouse decided to help. They wanted to give back. They started to donate to fix up that dingy old lighthouse. They upgraded all the equipment. They painted the building. They bought carpeting to cover the cold cement floor. And they cooked all day preparing a banquet for the rescuers.

It was a beautiful meal with all the fixings. The rescuers had never experienced such gratitude. Everyone was having a wonderful time celebrating life in the newly painted and upgraded lighthouse. There was only one problem. The claxon went off.

The rescuers flew out of the meal, donned their gear and headed for the sea, much to the offense of those who spent all day cooking, and many weeks planning.

The survivors from tonight's shipwreck dripped water and mud all over the new carpet. Worse, the rescuers had to give a couple victims CPR. As they started breathing again, as is common with drowning victims, they vomited out the sea water. All. Over. The. New. Carpet. The donors were quite upset.

Worse, the team lost a rescuer in the stormy surf that night, so everyone was in a foul mood. Some of the former survivors who'd previously been saved by that team member were very angry at the newcomers, that tonight's shipwreck had cost the life of their hero.

But the donors were very resourceful. They came up with lots of ways to "fix" the "problem."

- "We need to have another room where victims can be brought if they're messy until they get cleaned up."
- "All shipwrecks need to be scheduled during a reasonable time so they don't interfere with our planned activities."
- "We need safety standards so the rescuers don't sacrifice too much. The lighthouse should be a safe place."
- "We need a Board of Directors so our donations aren't wasted on just any random shipwrecks. We need to pick and choose the strategic shipwrecks."

The rescuers couldn't believe their ears. While they appreciated the many expressions of gratitude they'd recently received, they hadn't realized that they came with strings attached, the strings of expectations. Expectations set everyone up for offense. And offense justifies any bad behavior, including ending relationships.

The rescuers realized the donors just didn't understand the lighthouse's life-saving mission. They tried to explain it, over and over. But the donors would have none of it. They'd forgotten that they were once shipwrecked themselves.

Eventually, they had a lighthouse split. The donors built a much bigger and grander lighthouse inland, away from that nasty, stormy shore. It had lights and music and amazing food and shopping and programs. Lots of comfortable programs. It was a place where you could really feel good about yourself. But no life was ever saved within its walls.

The rescuers stayed with the old dingy lighthouse on the shore, where the shipwrecks were. The new paint began to peel, and the new carpet became stained.

But lives were continually dragged out of the ocean and saved there. Some went right back out in the water and drowned. Others, once saved, went to the inland lighthouse, because it was just so much better funded and had better programs. But others became rescuers themselves, sharing what they'd been given.

There was never a shortage of shipwrecks.

What are we, the Church, supposed to be?

Are we a lighthouse with a life-saving mission to reach people who have wrecked their lives on the rocks of sin in the fog of deception? Or are we a pristine environment where everyone is happy all the time, or at least pretends to be?

Is church a place where we welcome grieving people in crises? Or is it a place where we go to feel good about ourselves?

Are we willing to allow messy people in our churches to learn the ways of life? Are we willing to learn the ways of life ourselves? Or do we think, having now been saved, that we know it all?

I believe we are called by God to be his hands, feet, voice, and heart to a wounded world, inviting all into painful, scary, but life-giving transformation through intimacy with Jesus.

1 John 3:18

Dear children, let us not love with words or speech but with actions and in truth.

Practical takeaways from this chapter:

- It's easy to forget that we once needed rescue when we no longer need rescue.
- We are called to be Jesus' hands, feet, voice, and heart to a wounded world.

Because the church is a lifesaving station, not a live stage show.

Chapter 11:
3 mindset traps that hijack Jesus' mission to wounded people

As the Church, we are Jesus' hands, feet, voice, and heart to the world. We invite wounded people into transformational intimacy with our Savior by stewarding both compassion and truth well. But there are three mindset traps that hijack Jesus' mission to wounded people.

These three mindset traps are so sneaky we often don't realize we've fallen into them. But they can sweep whole churches away from their Kingdom calling and make them completely ineffective. Worse, these Christians (and even whole churches!) don't know they've been spiritually shipwrecked because (1) their metrics look so good to other humans, and (2) they are so busy.

So let's go through these three mindset traps. And then we'll talk about the mindset that the Church, and we as Christians, are called to have to effectively reflect Jesus to a wounded world, stewarding the hearts of wounded people well.

Mindset Trap #1: Empire Building

We fall into this one when we're more concerned about building our empire than we are about building the Kingdom of God. **If our goal is to have people swoon over** our personal importance and status, we've received our reward in full from the people we've impressed. We have none from God.

Matthew 6:1-6, 16-18

[1] "Be careful not to practice your righteousness in front of others to be seen by them. **If you do, you will have no reward from your Father in heaven.**

[2] "So when you give to the needy, do not announce it with trumpets, as the hypocrites do in the synagogues and on the streets, to be honored by others. Truly I tell you, **they have received their reward in full.**

[3] "But when you give to the needy, do not let your left hand know what your right hand is doing, [4] so that your giving may be in secret. Then your Father, who sees what is done in secret, will reward you.

[5] "And when you pray, do not be like the hypocrites, for they love to pray standing in the synagogues and on the street corners to be seen by others. Truly I tell you, **they have received their reward in full.**

[6] "But when you pray, go into your room, close the door and pray to your Father, who is unseen. Then your Father, who sees what is done in secret, will reward you.

[16] "When you fast, do not look somber as the hypocrites do, for they disfigure their faces to show others they are fasting. Truly I tell you, **they have received their reward in full.**

[17] "But when you fast, put oil on your head and wash your face, [18] so that it will not be obvious to others that you are fasting, but only to your Father, who is unseen; and your Father, who sees what is done in secret, will reward you." – Jesus (emphasize mine)

It's so easy to fall into this super-sneaky mindset trap because it looks so good on the outside. And often it started well, with good intentions, passionate hearts, and a legitimate calling from God.

But somewhere along the way, often very slowly, something shifted. The influence and importance became an end in itself. It became about the ministry, instead of about Jesus and the people he loves.

> **Galatians 3:3**
>
> **After beginning by the Spirit, are you now trying to finish by the flesh?**

Often, just from outside appearances, you can't tell the difference between one person building their own empire and another person walking out their calling and building the Kingdom in partnership with God. The actions can look the same. It's all about the motivations.

Here are some litmus tests to check our hearts to see if, and to what degree, we've fallen into empire building:

- We base ministry decisions on how they will affect our numbers (giving, attendance, etc.) rather than on how they will affect the hearts we minister to.

- We're not willing to do it for the one.

- The ROI (Return on Investment) is considered more than whether God is calling us to do the thing or not.

- We avoid making changes that will offend the biggest tithers.

- We believe the ends justify the means, compromising our integrity or principles for "the greater good" or "the greater purpose."

- In joint community events, we worry about which church, leader, or ministry gets the credit.

- Decisions are based on protecting our power, influence, and image rather than what God is calling us to do.

Very often empire builders are wounded people themselves, desperately medicating their own pain and insecurity by building a grand ministry. Often, Jesus lets the empire fall apart to bring them to the place of doing the hard work of addressing their own pain.

Matthew 7:21-23

[21] "Not everyone who says to me, 'Lord, Lord,' will enter the kingdom of heaven, but only the one who does the will of my Father who is in heaven. [22] Many will say to me on that day, 'Lord, Lord, did we not prophesy in your name and in your name drive out demons and in your name perform many miracles?' [23] Then I will tell them plainly, 'I never knew you. **Away from me, you evildoers!**' " – Jesus (emphasis mine)

> ### John 12:43
>
> They loved human praise more than praise from God.

Remember, Jesus chose and poured into 12 guys. He had lousy numbers. But his Kingdom impact changed the world.

Our numbers may look great in a presentation and get us approval and applause from people at conferences.

But if we're not stewarding well the hearts of people Jesus loves, then our numbers don't count for anything in Heaven.

Mindset Trap #2: Legacy Saving

Legacy savers care more about preserving institutional traditions than they do about moving with the Spirit of God. We've fallen into legacy saving when we prioritize preserving the church experience we grew up with above all else.

Although safe, comfortable, and familiar, such churches do not enable transformation. Transformation always involves change, so they shut it down. *Can't have the Holy Spirit coming in here and changing things!* But God's Kingdom is about saving lives, not legacies.

We know we're legacy saving when:

- We're afraid to make changes for fear of offending people.
- We have "sacred cows," emotional attachments to our things and our ways:
    - *"Don't move that picture! My grandmother donated that!"*
    - *"But we've always done it this way!"*
- We care more about preserving the church experience we grew up with than about evolving to reach the changing neighborhood around us.
- We hold on to things that used to work, but are no longer effective.
- There is anything that's not "on the table" to be cut if it interferes with reaching the region around us. The Bible calls these things "idols." Ouch!

The movie *Jesus Revolution* is a true story and a great example of a pastor (Chuck Smith, played expertly by Kelsey Grammer) deciding not to be a legacy saver. He opened up his church to the hippies in the early 1970s.

He paid a high price. He lost friends who had been in his church for decades. That had to hurt. But he gained so much more. He gained partnering with the manifest Kingdom of God in one of the greatest revivals the United States has ever seen.

"Sometimes the greatest opponents of what God is doing on the earth today are the guardians of what God did yesterday." – Arthur Burk

That doesn't mean traditions are bad. Traditions can connect us with the people of God who have gone before us. That's a good and beautiful thing.

But when a tradition interferes with reaching the community of wounded people around us, it becomes an idol and needs to go.

Mindset Trap #3: Compromising Truth

Law enforcement personnel use the term "winking" to describe ignoring illegal activities that we know are happening but, for whatever reason, choose not to deal with. A more common expression is "looking the other way." Sometimes people, governments, and yes, even churches, pretend either that a bad thing isn't happening or that it's really not that bad after all.

We "wink" at sin, compromising God's truth, when we condone, or don't speak out against, self-destructive and sinful lifestyles. Too often, the gospel's message of God's grace to all people has been hijacked as an excuse to make people feel good about themselves just the way they are, sin and all.

Yes, Jesus' message is "come as you are." You don't have to get all holy first before you come to Jesus. In fact, you can't.

But Jesus' message is never, "stay as you are." He invites us into life-changing transformation where we can no longer live sinful lifestyles that break his heart.

We know we've slipped into compromising truth when:

- We're afraid to say the word "sin."

- We pursue peace and unity at any price. Unity not centered on Jesus and his holiness is a false peace.

- We care more about offending the culture than we do about offending God.

- We condone, look the other way, or are even proud of lifestyles that are blatantly anti-Biblical and self-destructive.

When we don't identify sin as the self-destruction that it is, when we tell wounded people they aren't really wounded, **we slam the door of God's healing in people's faces.**

The Kingdom of God Mindset: Partnering with God

Yes,

- Numbers are important.
- It is right to honor our history.
- Everyone is welcome in the Kingdom of God.

But the mindset traps we've discussed take these legitimate concerns and twist them out of balance, into an end in themselves. And they are each motivated by fear.

The way out of all of these mindset traps is a single-minded focus on what God is calling us to do. As a Church. As an individual Christian. As a family. And the answer will be different for each church, each individual, and each family. Because none of us can do it all.

So let's trust and partner with God to do what he's calling us to do.

Then God will work all things together for the glory of his Kingdom. And that is the best possible outcome for us and everyone around us.

Practical takeaways from this chapter:

- If we are not stewarding hearts well, our numbers don't matter.

- Sometimes the greatest opponents of what God is doing today are the guardians of what God did yesterday.

- When we "wink" at self-destructive lifestyles, we slam the door of God's healing in people's faces.

- Partner with God to do what he's calling us to do.

Let's be willing to sacrifice:
- *Our importance and reputation.*
- *Our comfortable and familiar way of doing things.*
- *The approval of the culture and of others.*

Chapter 12:
7 practical tips to steward wounded hearts well

Learn to validate wounded people's pain.

As our world sinks deeper and deeper into depravity, our churches are going to be overwhelmed by a flood of hurting people. We need to get comfortable being around people who are hurting without trying to fix them.

Before trying to solve their problem or offering them help, there's something important we need to do first. And it makes all the difference.

> **The single most important thing you can do to help someone who's hurting is validate their pain.**

Before you do anything else, validate their pain. Validate how they feel. This gives them acceptance instead of judgment, and it creates a safe place.

So how do we do this? In conclusion, here are 7 practical tips to help us enable the healing transformation God wants to bring, based on what we've learned in this book.

1) Let wounded people hurt. Honor their process.

That sounds really strange, doesn't it? *Let them hurt?!?
That's not compassionate!* Let me explain. I don't mean

ignore them or their pain. I don't mean being cold or distant, indifferent or insensitive.

Here's the deal. When someone's going through their "Dark Night of the Soul," either physically, emotionally, or spiritually, we naturally want to find them an off-ramp. Out of compassion, we want to fix the problem for them. Don't do that, because you can't. Only Jesus is the healer.

> **Psalm 23:4 (NKJV)**
>
> Though I walk through the valley of the shadow of death, I will fear no evil; for You are with me; Your rod and Your staff, they comfort me.

Jesus doesn't pull us out of the "valley of the shadow of death." He walks with us through it. Don't try to pull them out. Be present with them in it.

2) Be present.

There is such a thing as the Ministry of Presence. Someone who is just willing to be present brings so much more healing than someone who thinks they have all the answers.

Just be there. Not with all the answers. Not with a "golden scroll" that dropped out of Heaven. Not with a paradigm-shifting solution that will magically make it all better for them.

Just be there.

You're just there for them, in whatever capacity, at whatever distance they need you to be.

A great question is, "How can I support you in this? What would bless you most?"

Now don't get me wrong. You're not giving them a blank check. If they ask for something you can't (or don't want to) provide, you are free to offer something else you are able and willing to provide.

But the point is you're present, without an agenda. They are not a project to be fixed. They are a person to be with.

3) Get comfortable with silence.

Think about it. Everything in our modern Western world is designed to protect us from one thing. Silence.

"I really need to spend some quiet, reflective time. I think I'll get on social media," said no one ever. If we're not careful, our lives can get driven by notifications: Someone reacted to my post! Text message! Look who added to their Instagram story! I got more followers!

I'm not knocking social media. It is a great communication tool, and it can be fun. It has its place. But we've inadvertently engineered ourselves into a world with no silence.

So when we're talking to someone who's hurting, we don't like an "awkward silence." So we break it too soon. But the wounded person needed that silence.

Silence is healing. They are processing in the silence, and if you break it too soon, you can rob them of what God is doing in that moment. Sometimes just waiting for them to form the words, however long it takes, speaks volumes more than anything you could have said.

They needed the silence that you broke too soon.

Waiting for someone to form the words in their own timing is incredibly honoring. And honor imparts healing. That's why just being comfortable with silence, letting the other person break it first, can be tremendously healing for them.

When you're trying to comfort someone who's hurting or grieving, don't be the one to break the silence. Let them break it when they're ready.

4) Have an abundance mindset.

People who love well are givers. They don't keep score. They don't say, "Well, you owe me now, because I helped you." Their love, help, and acceptance does not come with strings attached.

People committed to doing life together lift each other up, not tear each other down. They have an abundance mindset. No one is afraid of your success, and they even celebrate it.

A rising tide raises all boats.

Unhealthy, unsafe churches have a scarcity mindset. They think there's only so much success, or favor with God, to go around. So if you're successful, that means less success for them. In fact, they are actually afraid of your success. If you get too successful, or your life reflects too much of God's favor, they'll cut you back down to size.

> *There are no giants allowed*
> *in a kingdom of dwarves.*

You can see this play out in the leadership. Are the leaders in competition with each other? Are they guarded around each other? Or do they protect and affirm each other? Can they be safely vulnerable around each other?

Healthy churches are not made up of cookie-cutter people. They don't try to force everyone into the same mold. They aren't afraid of people's differences. They don't try to force everyone else to be like them. They celebrate the uniqueness that God placed in each individual. These are the safe people we can do life with.

5) Remind wounded people of their identity, not their shame.

As the Body of Christ, we should support people's healing journey, and not guilt them for admitting their struggles.

There's a village in Africa where, when a woman is pregnant, she goes into the forest with her friends until they get "the song of the child." Then they go back and teach it to the village.

The village sings the person's song at significant events in the person's life, like their birth, their death, when they kill the leopard, get promoted in the tribe, etc.

But they also sing the song when the person messes up, often in adolescence. This is the village's discipline. The tribe gathers around them and says, "You're not acting like yourself. Let us remind you of who you are." Then the village sings their song to them.

Please don't misunderstand the metaphor. The story is obviously not saying we bring people up front and shame them.

The point is the Church is supposed to support our true, God-given identity, by reminding us who we are and how Heaven sees us. And that's a beautiful picture.

It's a far cry from the common but unhealthy practices of:

- Holding someone "accountable" by holding them hostage through shame.
- Never saying anything to anyone about their lifestyle choices, no matter how self-destructive they are.

When we do life together, everyone is allowed to be in process. None of us have arrived. Everyone's contribution is valued. Everyone's calling is valued. No one is flippantly disqualified because of what they are going through.

6) You aren't the professional. You aren't Jesus. Don't try to be either.

Be their friend, not their counselor or their savior. You don't have to fix them. And, frankly, they don't want to be fixed. They want to be healed.

Don't try to be their savior; that's Jesus' job. Don't try to lead them through healing if:

1. You haven't received healing yourself, or
2. You don't know what you're doing.

Especially if they have been through trauma (emotional or physical abuse, sexual abuse, gaslighting, abortion, etc.) Don't try to be the professional when you aren't.

7) Advice requires permission. Ask first. Restore their voice by honoring their no.

Offer to help them find good help, whether it's pastoral or professional counseling, inner healing, or whatever resources their situation requires. Always ask first. Don't impose a solution. Instead, give them options and the freedom to not take your advice without condemnation or disappointment from you. They need to drive their healing, not you, although you can respectfully suggest possible routes.

There's nothing more rewarding than being a friend to someone in their time of need. There's nothing more rewarding than being there, not necessarily as the person with all the right answers, but just as the person who was there when they needed you.

Ask if you can help them find the right help. Asking is very important. Never impose a solution by saying things like:

- *"You should read this book."*
- *"Here's a counselor that deals with these issues."*

Get permission first. Ask first, like this:

- *"Would you like some resources to help with that?"*
- *"Would you like me to help you find a counselor (or pastor or ministry) who deals with that?"*

If they say yes, then you can ask them if they've read that book, or give them your ministry recommendation. Now you have their permission and you're not imposing one more thing on them. Now you're being truly helpful.

If they say no, then just drop it. I cannot emphasize this enough: **Honor. Their. No.**

Sometimes, especially with trauma victims, abuse was inflicted upon them by people stronger and in authority who did not hear, let alone honor, their no. Their voice was ignored and shut down.

So just saying, "Ok, no worries," and dropping your advice, honoring their no, is the most healing thing you can do for them. It restores their voice.

No matter how much you think your resource will help them, honor their no. They aren't ready for it yet. Keep it in your back pocket for another time when they're ready.

Wounded people won't let us help them until they know they won't be wounded more by doing so.

Practical takeaways from this chapter:
1. Let wounded people hurt. Honor their process.
2. Be present.
3. Get comfortable with silence.
4. Have an abundance mindset.
5. Remind wounded people of their identity, not their shame.
6. You aren't the professional. You aren't Jesus. Don't try to be either.
7. Advice requires permission. Ask first. Restore their voice by honoring their no.

By practicing these 7 practical things, we create a safe place for wounded people to receive healing.

Conclusion:
How to Steward Wounded Hearts Well

By stewarding well the wounded hearts of people Jesus loves, we reflect his heart to a wounded world that desperately needs him, a world trying so hard to medicate their pain with everything else.

To recap the skills you've learned in this book:

- How to validate their pain by learning what to say and what not to say (Chapters 1 and 2).
- How to receive their story with compassion and not judgment (Chapter 3).
- How to recognize shame without doing more damage (Chapter 4).
- How to understand woundedness and trauma (Chapters 5 and 8).
- How to help support someone who's working through forgiving something hard by helping them grieve the loss (Chapters 6 and 7).
- How to restore someone's voice by honoring their no (Chapter 9).
- How to view the Church as a lifesaving station (Chapter 10).
- Avoid the 3 mindset traps that hijack our ministry to wounded people (Chapter 11).

- Practice 7 practical tips for creating a safe place and becoming a safe person (Chapter 12).

This is how we, as Jesus' hands, feet, voice, and heart in the world, can support wounded people who need us. This is how we make our churches safe places for people in crisis. And we'll be grateful for that safe place in our time of need.

So are you willing to steward wounded hearts well? What an awesome thing to be trusted by God with the heart of another! May we prove trustworthy.

Because if they can't go to the people of God when they're hurting, where can they go?

If this book was useful to you…

Please leave a 5-star review on Amazon. This is a powerful thing you can do to help this message reach more people. And it only takes a few minutes.

A good review only needs a few sentences and answers three questions:

The first sentence answers the question, "Why did I almost *not* buy this book?"

Then a few sentences answer the question, "How was this book useful to me?" This can be just one sentence, but it could be two or three. The more concise, the better.

Finally, the last sentence answers the question, "What would I say to someone on the fence?"

For your convenience, here is a QR Code (and link) that redirects straight to the Amazon review page for this book:

IdentityInWholeness.com/swh-reviews

Acknowledgements

Nothing worthwhile is ever accomplished alone. Here are just a few of the significant people who helped this book become a reality.

Thank you Rob Fitzpatrick, Devon Hunt, Brian Hall, and the whole UsefulBooks.com community, who taught me how to write a useful non-fiction book. Thank you for building a useful community!

Thank you to the 60+ beta-readers who helped me fix the book's problems before it was published, gave over 1400 useful comments in 3 rounds of beta-reading, some great endorsements, and helped me measure when it was actually ready to publish. Working with you was my favorite part of this whole process!

And thank you to the HelpThisBook.com team for creating such a great beta-reading tool.

Thank you, Lindsay Sutton, a.k.a. *The Comma Killer*, for your fantastic job of copy-editing.

A special thank you to Janet, my lovely wife, for your support for yet another of my crazy ideas. Here's to the adventure!

And most of all, thank you, Lord Jesus, for the calling you put on my life. Thanks for never giving up on me.

Free Resources

Here are some additional, free resources, applications of the concepts in this book to real-world situations. I hope you find them useful.

Accountability is a dumpster fire. Download this free resource to learn 4 reasons why accountability doesn't work and how to build a compassionate, truthful community instead.

IdentityInWholeness.com/accountability

Post-abortive healing is not about the politics. It's about the humans. Download this free resource to learn about post-abortive trauma and 5 ways to become a safe place for post-abortive people.

IdentityInWholeness.com/post-abortive-humans

About the Author

Dave grew up in Los Angeles, CA. He graduated from UCLA with a master's degree in mathematics, into a day job with computers.

Dave has a strong affinity for all parts of the Body of Christ, including the Evangelical, Catholic and Charismatic traditions.

The Lord has held Dave close through much brokenness and loss. Through it all, God provided divine inner healing, miraculous relationship restorations, and His tremendous, incredibly close presence, with more to come.

Dave and his wife Janet live in Fredericksburg, VA. They are passionate about sharing the healing they've received and seeing the Church walking in wholeness as the Bride of Christ we are called to be. They facilitate inner healing in their local church and volunteer with Rachel's Vineyard, a post-abortive trauma recovery ministry in Richmond, VA, for both women and men.

Please email Dave at dave@IdentityInWholeness.com.

Visit their website at IdentityInWholeness.com.

Detailed Section Index

- 126 -

If this book was useful to you…

Please leave a 5-star review on Amazon. This is a powerful thing you can do to help this message reach more people. And it only takes a few minutes.

A good review only needs a few sentences and answers three questions:

The first sentence answers the question, "Why did I almost *not* buy this book?"

Then a few sentences answer the question, "How was this book useful to me?" This can be just one sentence, but it could be two or three. The more concise, the better.

Finally, the last sentence answers the question, "What would I say to someone on the fence?"

For your convenience, here is a QR Code (and link) that redirects straight to the Amazon review page for this book:

IdentityInWholeness.com/swh-reviews